CW01510357

SHADOW SONG

———

OTHER BOOKS

Unnumbered Pages

SHADOW SONG

FRANCIS GALLAGHER

Published in 1993 by
Francis Gallagher
36 Mavisbank Gardens
Bellshill ML4 3ES
Scotland

© Francis Gallagher 1993

*This book is copyright. No part of it may be reproduced in any form without
permission in writing from the publishers except by a reviewer who wishes
to quote brief passages in connection with a review written for inclusion in a
newspaper, magazine, radio or television broadcast.*

British Library Cataloguing in Publication Data

A catalogue record for this book is available from the British Library

ISBN 0 9520259 0 6

Designed and Produced by Images Design and Print Ltd
Printed and Bound in Great Britain by Hartnolls Ltd, Bodmin, Cornwall.

To Peter and Ellen

ONE HUNDRED HAIKU

———————————

eternal Nippon

cerulean sky

above the sea of days

like Fred Astaire

the rain tap dances

as it drops from the eaves

at midnight

the horses are nodding off

in the field

like an army shaking its spears

the grass waits an order

from general wind to attack

the thousand turns

a river takes

before the final sea

fall of a single leaf

announces the arrival

of autumn every where

in the morning snow

tracks of small animals

the scratched epitaph

of those who die in the night

like a sneak thief

the wind breaks into a garden

steals what he can

autumn moon

so beautiful its overflow

beautifies the rest

and the fallen branch

leave it there for it

belongs to the forest

it is not your switch

winter trees

hedgehogs

on stilts –

the fallen leaves

like the faces of gamblers

all their money gone

waiting for the next wind to blow

an elderly tea lady

rushed off her feet

flushed autumn moon

the mountain range

a family sitting down to a meal

cloudy menus

ouch the little waves cry

when the blades of the reed cutters

slip and wound them

after a storm

the strangeness of ordinary things

arranged in a different way

after the storm

quiet as nature

buries its dead

like a nagging wife

the wind whines all night

no divorce though it's catholic

a last sting of summer when

like a faithful samurai the

bee injects his poison then

follows his master to death

trees gossip in a wind bending

over like women across a fence

they must be talking about sex

now because they're whispering

one more cherry blossom fell

than was absolutely necessary

it is already winter

snow in July

a field of daisies

and too much sake

across a garden's throat

the clothes rope becomes

a necklace of rain drops

whiplash wind smacks

the farmer's face

like a woman's libber

a snake of wind

crosses the field

strikes the heel of the peasant

with poisonous cold

an old married couple

the wind and tree quarrel all day

to see who'll give up first

the felled trees

dead samurai

never to rise again

when the wind hass passed

the corn field straightens its hem

like a woman re arranging her skirt

something is missing

in a field a scare

crow has fallen over

like beautiful women

the scare crows note

what each is wearing

the solitary crow

flies off when another bird

alights on the tree

the emptiness resonates

when a single crow

flies across the field at dusk

like Robinson Crusoe

the crow on a tree

surrounded by snow

against the snow

a morse code of crows

the message is

it's bloody cold

the crow scans the field

like a sour old teacher his class

if anything moves he'll kill it

crow in the falling snow

was there any warm part to him

he'd freeze to death

a dirty old glove

the crow flies up gracefully

1 thing each does well

crow on a dyke

conducts a symphony

of wind among the corn

even dusk holds back

on the rim of hills

till the bush warbler

has finished its song

when the weary traveller

hears the bush warbler

the world is not so desolate and thin

the call of the bush warbler
dissolves the anger
that scumily gathers about the heart

summer is over
when the bush warbler's call
has grown harsh
peevishness marks the end of things

wild geese
flying over the sea
the unheard fall
of the one who does not make it

like a bell
ringing silently
the butterfly
rising in the air

the mountains fall silent

but a frog starts up

like a fond Pavarotti

birds sheltering from the rain

in the branches of a tree like

the regulars of a pub each one

perched in his accustomed seat

a spaceship among the stars

the butterfly flies

from garden to garden

an arrow of moving water

the rat closes in on its target

a mother counts her chicks in despair

don't sing too loud
little bird
the cat too
is a music lover

a bird on a tree
watching for winter
when it comes he will leave
the last wave of spring

a black snowball
a dirty sparrow
quarrelling with the air
as he bundles along

black snow
falling sideways
a flock of starlings

the flight of birds

and smoke of morning

leave no trace at noon

cut grass crow hunts worms

at every turn of the world

it's prey or predator time

the seagulls

over the rubbish dump

are no longer graceful

not like the chariot race

in Ben Hur

the frogs drifting

on the duckweed

the wet morning

is a distant bell

tolling disconsolately

exhausted like a chess master

playing many different people at once

the day gives up

and concedes defeat of numbers

the half winds stirs the boughs

finally even an afternoon ends

time to drink watch television

old women talking

dinosaurs discussing what it was

that killed them

counting out my life the

raindrops from the eaves

the ticks of a mad clock

the 2 hardest lives to live

one another chooses for you

and one you choose yourself

like the rain

life says nothing

it just goes on

till it stops

when nothing happens

the tears of life

fall instead

quiet panic at the heart

when your own generation

starts dying death knows

your name where you live

mother and aunts dead

no one says put on a scarf

going out so you don't get a cold

a mother's death

is the hardest thing

you could not live through

another such day

easier to recall an arrow

than take back a word

spoken to hurt one we love

small boats at their moorings then
leaving early or late so unnoticed
a face absent from the usual scene

thining too much about the past
makes you cry at lost
pleasure and lost pain too
if that was it or you

the letter box rattles
letters of love success you think
but it's the snap of the house
falling on emptiness

why is it when we see a friend
we haven't met for some time
and who hasn't noticed us we think
twice about going up to him

heaven and hell

we build for ourselves

from good and evil

we choose our own souls

the thin rain

that falls on autumn afternoons

sums up my life so far

the last bird

to sing at twilight

finds an answering chord in me

picking up a magazine

it falls open naturally

at my own work

let us separate
so that we never meet
if not lovers
then perfect strangers

we live and die
without ever really
knowing what we think
too afraid to find out

even the introvert's car
doesn't like to be parked
beside other cars

1 is unbearable
2 is almost bearable
3 is politics
4 is war

Shadow Song

the great philosopher
is suddenly lost
when a speck of dust
gets in his eye

in the mixed sauna
every one trying not
to give each other marks
out of ten for anatomy

at mid night in a parked car
adulterers discuss their affair
they mean to end it but somehow can't

a wasted day
not quite for at midnight
I wrote a haiku

if you meet Basho

throw him in the pond

with that ****** frog

the houses at midnight

are like skulls set on

the shelf in catacombs

the alcoholic gravedigger

drunk on his bike

will need his own services soon

on the library book

fingerprint of the last reader

what I wonder was his crime

most of the things

you say you can't do

most of the things

you do you can't say

the white snake of dawn

uncurves itself on the horizon

is the day venomous or not

the moon through the bare trees

in a crowd seeing lives

I might have lived

the dark barked all night

must have been in love

some bitch ruined another life

greedy fish swallows a hook

the first step to perdition

is when you open your mouth

going for an afternoon sleep

when I awoke

summer was over

dew turns to thorn

the briefness of things

what hurts most of all

I watch the morning

gather in its little crowd of life

like a mother hen her chicks

and some will go astray

like a rare animal in the zoo

the sales assistant in the shop

no one can afford to go in to

north of shadows

life lasts a moment

then it's gone

a bird's shadow

flickers across the room

the sadness of time passing

no matter how cut or abused

the bamboo always grows back

just like the people

PROLEGOMENA

Shadow Song

if I was starting out tomorrow

I'd write nothing but Mills & Boons

make a calculated 50,000 a year

retire to a villa in topless Spain

poetry gives you a headache

art has done nothing for me

I'd rather have the money instead

that's what I honestly feel

writing's just an obsession too strong to break now

where do the words come from

well at birth you get the type of brain

that responds to verbal stimulus and

your childhood makes you into a loner

then a fantasist or psychological realist

existentially sick writing was the only thing

you could do/cared about being so screwed up

and that my friends is the origin of great art

as if I should know still interesting the insights of losers

Shadow Song

I think people are writers

so they can act as crazy as they feel

poets are expected to be weird perverted oddballs

I think you always felt strange and

writing is a hook to hang that perceived difference on

also being an artist entitles you to make a mess

of your life but call that material

such are the personal myths we live by

did you ever have that feeling

of defeated design a person/meeting not

followed through the afterwards felt the miss

inevitable the gap iconic well that's how I feel

about my life expectations not materializing

a sense the whole thing was never on anyway

the loss and non ness of it becomes the chief reality

yes non occurrence is the ironic truth of our existence

Shadow Song

disappointing when the postman fails to call

the rage of absence nothing is infectious you feel you don't exist

when you receive no letters are not even remembered

by people you send money to the desperate

are those who live for the second post

that perfumed note of love white letter of success

they don't come of course and you realize

that's what your life was waiting for some thing not to happen

don't talk to me about love

you think someone is obsessed with you

and she hardly knows you exist you think

people need you but they can do without or

pay for it love is being necessary to someone

the great passions of autumn the last throw

of the desperate dice are not about love or sex

but the wormy fear of loneliness

Shadow Song

love after all is only possible between strangers

to know somebody well excludes a monistic emotion

every thing genuine is streaked with otherwise

of course you start by loving people for their good points

then discover their real identity lies in their bad ones

in the end you have to love their weaknesses

not mythic strengths feelings drift rift so love is

the ability to forgive others disappointing us as

we forgive our own disappointing selves

all people really want is miracles

perfect sex to make him young again

reinstate life chances love to make her beautiful

it doesn't work out like that people settle for marriage

a bourgeois bargain negotiated space contract

of the managerial society dissolvable if not fulfilled and not

the biggest sexual disease is unreasonable expectations

starting tomorrow people will get married 3 or 4 times

a spouse for each turning point or never marry at all

in the future there will be no middle only extremes

I hate it when people make promises

then don't keep them say they'll write or call

have you waiting days/years then don't come

even omit to apologize so what was a big event

in your humble life was merely a footnote of forgetting

for them or failing that they actually come through

and there's some fumbled attempt at intimacy

sexual or intellectual and after they leave you wonder

why you just can't get close to people

and the unbridgeable distance between desire and its occasions

Prolegomena

the dog next door craps in my garden

the man next door spreads rumours about me

you could live this life for a thousand years

and you'd still have nothing to show for it

I wish I could leave this nothing town and shitty little country

and the cold rain of wind blown afternoons

go some where warm and sexy you often feel

another kind of unhappiness and failure is the most

or best you can hope for just let it start before it's too late

Shadow Song

Modern Sonnets: 1
it's hard just the same when you find
out that the western hero of your childhood
was a free ranging homosexual dude
who shacked up with the villain and

the saloon girl's gowns looked better on him than her
I mean what's left to believe in after that
screwing the fat guy in the black hat
fighting in the leading lady's underwear

where do you go in life to get your money
back for having all the wrong illusions
the cowboy habitue of homo pornos
the code of the west in satin lingerie

how many took the cheap Hollywood heroics seriously
and got killed trying to be the hero in reality

Modern Sonnets: 2

modern life is like a mansion that has
been recently vacated but there's still in it
a sense of the previous tenants a definite
existential tone in the cold and empty house

as for modernism itself that is being stranded
between a past that is quickly dying out
and a future that cannot come to fruition
living between the abortive and the moribund

what I do myself is to begin from nothing
as if writing the first of every thing with
no morality and no politics like a witness
at a disaster taking notes and reporting

we cannot renew civilization or create a new one
what's left is the affrighted sanity of just holding on

Shadow Song

Modern Sonnets: 3

on a cool summer's afternoon with the

doors wide open you half hear the voices

of your dead and look up as if expecting to see

them coming in then but it's only the

children in the park neighbours in gardens

just as well both sides would be disappointed

our dead sorry at the way we had turned out

we resentful at their subsequent baneful influences

on us for at the end you've really got nothing

to say to the people you live with the silence

of mutual error exhaustion of false expectation it is

a dead draw love and hurt they merge to the stasis of

                                                    diminished being

we have a trade off with our dead the life

we live we do not believe the life we believe we do not live

Modern Sonnets: 4

freedom is not a good thing in itself

it is only good in what it might lead to

of course it is most conducive to the better life

yet freedom can also mean being free to do

social evil in the east the poetry of samizdat

is replaced by the slackness of pornography

the worth of words is succeeded by what

the nudes and the rightists bourgeois democracy

is a choice of which groups must suffer

for the air of prosperity usually the oldest

the sick unskilled in the selfishness of gold fever

economic freedom results in many casualties

on the march to prosperity those who can't keep up

will be left behind to die in the general disrupt

Shadow Song

Contemporaries

you remember them as carefree school boys

apprentice rebels against religion monogamy

etc then meet them in their sombre 30's

sober suited head teachers in the money

30 grand a year playing with their computer

like negro jazz pianists only to day

stern advocates of religion monogamy & the other

etcs like the last Roman senator at bay

keeping back the barbarian hordes

life plays some dirty tricks on you

you think you are going to be one person

but turn out some one else & opposite too

oh well not to worry we are the superfluous

any harm or good we can do is entirely circuitous

the stone in the stream

it is in other people that we see the full roll

effect and passage of time you remember her

a skinny kid crying mostly then from carrying a doll

to larking about in the front seat of her boyfriend's car

telling him to stop it with an encouraging smile

then with 2 young kids she's prematurely serious

finally she moves away to the richer life

of else where you're reduced to spectator status

as if life is what happens to others you have

been disqualified entered the solid stasis of decay's fold

thrown back on some thing in yourself that isn't enough

what is any thing compared to our getting old

not seen in the street signifies your death

until then being at the mercy of repetition's the

the sottish life

in the toilets at John o'Groats some underclass

scion scratched F---- THE POPE on the wall

and they ask why some of us are not populists but refuse

to find the plebs so deeply characterful and natural

of course worship of the working class is a strictly

bourgeois illusion the proles hate each other make

money to get away and never once ask specifically

to be patronised by socialist intellectuals not that it makes

any difference historically the working class is over

economically negligible the top slot in to the bourgeois

the bottom drop into welfare the rump left over

can't provide the basis of a politics or art or even a pose

in Scotland sentiment and emotion have the same force as

fact till they collide with the real world then roll over into bathos

internal exile

the hasp of society is broken no decent manners

or treatment all the time you feel you are being

lied to cheated treated with contempt by invisible centres

of malignancy your only purpose in life is cash dispensing

and at ground level neighbours don't talk to one

another the foreground cracks in divorce there is no back-

ground focus and the final alienation is not

having a relationship with yourself and unimaginable blank

is what we live nothing sustains itself social entropy doesn't

permit the promised utopias of tomorrow there are no

collectives to redeem race or class we are isolated economic units

with nothing in common but agreed moments of mutual

                                    temporary exploitation

contracts replace humanness but the art of the false

becomes more necessary to give people emotions they can't get

                                    from their own lifes

Shadow Song

the barbarians have reached the suburbs

each time you look the scum is getting higher

the video generation weaned on porno violence

kids swearing talking dirty drinking gutter monsters

of indiscipline invading your space intimidating you into silence

millions too afraid to go out at night for fear

of being burgled or attacked in the street

the climate of anxiety days being out of kilter

the red tide of anarchy laps about your feet

all quality gone the underclass take over society

how can democracy survive when the wasters

and criminals form a legitimate majority

no morality no taboo no escape from social predators

a new dark ages emanates from the United States of

America the wars of the future the suburb against the ghetto

autumnal confessions

OK I admit it you can burn me at the stake of the

ideological inquisition but I am getting more rightist with

the years West Indians I find surly aggressive is there

some where else they can go Asian fundamentalists I wish

would emigrate to Iran if that is where pure religion

is lived gays I find a pain in the arse (no pun meant)

such serious penises now but the very worst legion

of all feminists and their politics of rabid resentment

I guess you're middle aged when you can't stand

women and find socialism an illusion the world doesn't

need somehow along the way you run out of sympathy and end

with no friends no lovers only the caught randomness of moments

it will be interesting to see how this generation dies

is life made more or less precious by seeming to be such shallow lies

Shadow Song

the final form

so disappointing the final form

our lives take a job woman pension

trivial the things you end up living for

esp. after the legend of me & giant expectation

pain of comparison the things you were

going to achieve the little done did life once

play for you look to run in your favour

or all the same however we threw the dice

enfeebled might have been the missed

telephone call the letter that didn't reach

look/knock not answered difference now if we'd

responded positively to the first approach

so rolls on disappointment's iron tide

proper if onlys or were we always going to be on the losing side

short goodbyes

in life now the mad search is on

to find a substitute for the faded essence

of existence poetry sex self obsession

books won't constitute a saving instance

then the summer of being 40 and hours

knock like a drunk on your door

you lie back ltake it all as whores

too old poor to refuse the anything that's there

what is is you settle for finally

the comfort of the ditch gloss of performance

just getting through the day technically

being well off vice's cowardly balance

the longer we exist the more the primal loss

what kills is the lack of myth and telos

Shadow Song

when love is going well then on one

quite looks like your love nor

can any thing resemble what she owns

but when love has broken down

every passing female serves to recall

some part of her that was beautiful

every other car or object envisions

one of her personal possessions

nothing is ever like success where

as every thing is alike in failure

when you try to put the past behind

fragments of miss torture your mind

haunted by the deeper life you'd have lived

if only we had been truly loved

Borges

what should I have in common

with philosophers and flowers

but the strange necessity of having

to die and leave it all behind

as if one had ever understood

or possessed it even once

for us he panic isn't death

but fear of never having lived

absence of depth haunts our lives

the thin experience sex represents

irony going into the blankness

not finding who or what we were

in a culture obsessed with self

nothing further off than its realization

Shadow Song

life

life's like a dull party

full of boring people

sad to stay but

sadder still to leave

you might miss some thing

love

how much we could use them

now all those gifts of love

we gave to people who proved

unworthy so doubling the loss then

sex

in his love making

traces of every other woman

he has known

which part is me she wonders

poetry

not believing some thing I read

in a poem but then an action of

my life verifies it and I am as

pleased as if I'd seen my grave

politics

yes these are strange times

when each conversation ends

with the death of socialism

the last dinosaur after all

Shadow Song

and all those years

where did they go

vanished now like snow

leaving nothing but tears

somehow and don't ask me about it

you manage just to scrape through

each living day of it but without

ever being sure why or how you do

like birds that call to each other

in the hour before dawn or at dusk

souls cry out for love but no one can hear

so their beautiful song turns to dust

embarrassed now to meet a former colleague

for despite all that was said or threatened

nothing happened the status quo deepened and

in the ditch of sameness both spent another age

in a city of several million

you might not ever find

one good friend or one

true lover to the insufficient end

of the odds sods and demi gods

the last break first the first

break at mid point so the sods

are left to hold the line just

Shadow Song

If all this is allowed going

on the gaining in 1991

what will it be like in 2021

when people are 30 times as bad again

                    the past that existed too much

                    seems unreal to us now and

                    the future that did not happen as such

                    remains uppermost in our mind

the whores of satire make more money

than their targets but then the rich always

want to feel good about themselves ratly

gnawing at each other scores both ways

Agatha Christie

old age a murder book

reading itself to see

on the last page what

it was that killed it

if you kept all of life's little bits

that you throw away or use wastefully

there would be enough of the stuff to

make an almost complete other 1 of it

Shadow Song

figures in a dream

a stained and creased pack

of cards being shuffled for the millionth

time the Monday morning faces of the

robotic crowd going to work

hearing some one maligned in gossip

as the owner of a spectacular vice

and tho a complete stranger you know

that mentioned man to his inmost soul

where the human ends art begins

tho hating you out of foiled love

the power of what is to come will forgive

for the poem's hurt origins

some days in the crowd

you see your past your

future and think every

one's dying today with

some kind of addiction

how long can this last

so after the accident you say

go some other time some other

road think some other thought

be someone else and live some

other life so it does not all

gather at 1 point of disaster

only too late for changes now

Shadow Song

weak days

Sundays of weakly thinking about sin

then it's only Monday and I'm already done in

then thin neutral Pharisaical Tuesday's trope

then restless Wednesday full of limited scope

then dark Thursdays of grimly hanging on

and Friday of coming through the great persecution

then divine Saturday that is 2 days worth

of rest voracious release and end to dearth

then starting all over again you

think it's impersonal time that's

passing like a shadow now through

the gate but it's your life that's passed

and as the distance turns to go

it leaves the trampled silences of snow

by afternoon the world is pinched to slush

and people giving it one last middle aged push

Let me explain my soul to you

in these days of desire:

you ask me now because I'm old

and afraid of being even older

and you you are not so young

that in the toils of waiting

might not flourish a prolific decay

you will not then be the beauty

you are today and any way I feel

I've waited long enough for sexual

love before the sex was over

with itself or love never grew to lover

in you it's all come together

the desire the love the perfect other

but too tired to bargain & too fragile

to be tested time does not smile

on me any more so come now or not

Shadow Song

at all tomorrow I won't care for the lot

of it a thing is true in its frame

if it doesn't happen loses its name

today I love you more than anything

1 more day of unacted love you'll be nothing

Moments: 2

listen intense off centre people like us have

only chance for we're like desperate frighten

refugees trying to cross a closed border

we can carry nothing trivial or surplus only

our skin and the nakedness of understanding in

line with that we must tell each other the truth

of what we think and feel and want and are no

holding back no polite evasion no mind reading

games (nothing destroys love so much as tests

of love) unless we know the exact weight and

lack of one an other we will not get through

never make it to that other country where exiles

will feel at home in for the obstacles are for-

midable searchlights barbed wire gun emplacements

the watchtowers and the dogs the remoseless

guards of the frontier the pitiless killing

ground where most things founder and everything

will seem designed to stop us and even having

Shadow Song

broken through told every thing there may be

nothing there but a smiling ironic desert we

might be police spies after all agents pro-

vocateurs or just material or a poem over

when written or there as bad as here or zero

to survive for no last illusion to cling to

but life is a choice of risks a gambler's last

throw through the minefield of the future the

most dangerous path is the safest shall we

make love's sojourn into a run for the border

and the created life of two do we dare do we

doomsday now

one day we'll kill

all the animals and

be alone in the still

silence of an end

yet the irony of life

without other forms human

existence can't be itself

but runs to ragged ruin

Shadow Song

real life

it's curious how some thing

(usually prejudiced and trivial)

that you are told when young

sticks in your mind and soul

like spars wedged in rock and

tho' you know the thing itself

isn't true it becomes the end

sum of what you know of life

worse feel a weird duty to give

it on to the next generation

in sick insistence they relive

your mistakes and its pain

the arrogance of failure

all anything is but oppressive

to influence one or the future

our record is not so impressive

Salon des Refusés

this poem was withdrawn

because it wasn't left wing enough

it wasn't pseudo working class

it didn't support women ism

it didn't advance racial

minorities not having the correct

attitudes its crimes were endless

and it was written by a male

white middle aged middle class person

are there still some of these bastards

around hard to believe it now

yes in the politics of resentment

if you're not perfect you've got to go

the tribunal of the pure say so

cultural intimidation is necessary to balance

thousands of years of oppression with the same

OK when we do it prejudice if any one else does it

ideological war has been declared

fuck you if you are not one of the elect

this is printed on 100% re-cycled paper

Shadow Song

strange how you go

from being close friends

to people who say hello

is that how it ends

with a half smile and

a cool heart after such

intimacy change's rend

you don't have much

to show for your life

love mostly fails

friendship's abortive

long palls short falls

the fragility of the human

we try to conceal

but it does all hang

by a thread of unravel

a rift drift shift

redraws the emotional scene

ones we'd die for shit

we don't like even

there's a moral there

only give what you won't

miss can recall odds are

it's the impure loss of want

should keep your energy

for yourself or some thing

singular like art the day

shared comes to nothing

should be consistent

you'll have to face

death alone the last moment

is the truth of every race

Shadow Song

the brilliant talkers

and who remembers now all the brilliant talk

apercus maxims put downs switch back

paradox so sexy at the time that in the room

the beautiful women fell silent to listen to him

what ever became of those star talkers

alcohol legend disease biographers

raked them over tho' in the cold print

the words had lost the vigour of their mint

and who survived came through and got it down

where it mattered in inky black renown

the water drinking bore in the corner

making notes with his eyes among the febrile glitter

the one who asks the ugliest woman in the place

and got knocked back to his face

while nothing of the marvellous talk remains

he at least got a novel for his pains

and those who held the crowd with eloquence

have faded and passed from the garrulous scene

but subtle revenge of the obscure quiet observer

to give them their character too silent now to enter any other

Shadow Song

2 o'clock in the morning

3 things that make you
feel lonely in the night

the song of the birds
that goes on till the dawn

the noise of goods wagons
shunting in the distance

the laughter of lovers
saying goodnight to each other

these make you taste your loneliness
like the fish feels the iron

question of the hook in its mouth
and you wonder what it's

all in aid of when
it goes on like this

a false wind

the summer crowd gathers

they're open and bright as flowers

I feel autumn in my hand

like trees shivering in the wind

to be old is to feel it's all

been a false step and to tremble

twice at everything once for the life

you live once for the life you don't live

and is there still time for

all the present lacks or

the question a sign of ends

asking when it's too late for amends

life cheats it obscures goads

you to ignore the cry of crossroads

the postponed moment missed call

was your life chances after all

what you took for a casual wind

was the future leaving you behind

Shadow Song

it's sad to feel your life too much

a phone is ringing in an empty room

and you feel a vast irritation that

some one does not answer it or that

the person phoning does not hang up

or that someone else is called when

you are not or just the ugly noises

of common occurrences it is strange

how a mundane fractional event does

make you feel so intensely and in a

way whose effect you so much resent

is your life the sum of such things

a low accumulation of futile detail

we hate a thing that reminds us too

much of ourselves and wait in dread

for the phone to ring out again etc

the final fate

it is as if the dead people in

those old photographs knew that

one day some one would be looking

at them for their faces seem to state

between the casual laughter and

the solemn pose this is all that

these lives came to the guttered end

and you too occupy the same frame of fate

for the bird of death has already

taken flight whose shadow

will sweep over you and suddenly

in fear you look beyond the photo

as if people are examining your

picture in the family album a face

no one can identify now so you're

thrown away as not worth the space

Shadow Song

things seen at an angle or

the peculiar province of the low

contain for us an element of terror

for that is how you too will go

Lockerbie: the easy war

they are arrivals that will never be made now

and departures that will go on for ever

the relatives will look up stupidly tomorrow

for their loved ones to come in then remember

they were all sacrificed to some impossible cause

for terror is the last throw of socialism

the Aztec god that demands blood as release

and revenge for how final its own defeat is

on flight 103, the 259 victims of history

complete innocents caught in the brutal crossfire

of fanatics whose whole way of life is arbitrary

slaughter the injustice of death and evil's laughter

German police playing their own game lost the way

to hide their incompetence let the terrorists

slip through the net the purpose of security

is to conceal your own mistakes at any costs

Shadow Song

mad Gadaffi cranks his socialist revolution

the old man of the mountain in his terror state

sends out assassins to murder women and children

another moslem victory the intolerant religion of death & hate

and after the numbness of rage the self anger

loss of life blisters the waste of opportunity

all that putting off telling showing the other

how much you care as if you had eternity

and now you would sell your soul to recall

the dead even for a moment to tell them

all that's in your heart hardest of all

you'll both die without saying you love them

the crimes of history require the participation of too many

and for that reason no one is punished no one is guilty

light casualties

Sunday afternoon and he had it all planned

like a military operation up at eleven

breakfast then down to the pub and

back at 3 to see the war on television

a real war film during the dull stretches

of old blimps talking reads the supplement

nods off into fantasies of fighting and sex

wishes he was a soldier for the crumpet

the fight goes too well turns to a rout

mad with ambition all beneath the burning sun

a momentary hitch ensued but

with medals and promotion to be won

some stupid bastard of an officer

calls up an american air strike and

got a gungho high on glory flier

anxious to kill before the battle's end

Shadow Song

prove america is right and works

and warn tomorrow's enemy

maybe wishes it was ghetto blacks

only death can save the US of A

can boast to his kids back home

how daddy defeated AYRAB brutality

a real hollywood top gun kids that's me

so many heroes make an atrocity

rockets his own side off course blue on blue

the army's so poetical about death

only 9 killed casualties light that are not you

a small price for the greatest show on earth

6 teenagers their blood and skin like vandal

spray paint inside the carrier

death the human point where the arrogance

of computer killing breaks down and

the ancient slaughter takes over then

the knock on the door at midnight

to be told you have one less son

you might think victory too dearly bought

armchair heroes watch it on the painless screen

Britain is great again the old die in droves

at winter but thank god we're still men

who have the beating of inferior natives

we've destroyed the bastard of Baghdad he said

with hardly any of our side dead

goes out to celebrate a great British victory

while word of the incident reaches each family

Shadow Song

britain is a failed third rate island

off Europe with a flaky economy &

england can only appear a player

by being the fart of america's arse

what they died for england's illusion

that she exists the fancy dress nation

good at parades lives for client status

of the yanks and an invite to the important conferences